JUNE 2017

Afghanistan and Its Central Asian Neighbors

Toward Dividing Insecurity

AUTHOR
Ivan Safranchuk

A REPORT OF THE
CSIS RUSSIA AND EURASIA PROGRAM

CSIS | CENTER FOR STRATEGIC &
INTERNATIONAL STUDIES

ROWMAN & LITTLEFIELD
Lanham • Boulder • New York • London

About CSIS

For over 50 years, the Center for Strategic and International Studies (CSIS) has worked to develop solutions to the world's greatest policy challenges. Today, CSIS scholars are providing strategic insights and bipartisan policy solutions to help decisionmakers chart a course toward a better world.

CSIS is a nonprofit organization headquartered in Washington, D.C. The Center's 220 full-time staff and large network of affiliated scholars conduct research and analysis and develop policy initiatives that look into the future and anticipate change.

Founded at the height of the Cold War by David M. Abshire and Admiral Arleigh Burke, CSIS was dedicated to finding ways to sustain American prominence and prosperity as a force for good in the world. Since 1962, CSIS has become one of the world's preeminent international institutions focused on defense and security; regional stability; and transnational challenges ranging from energy and climate to global health and economic integration.

Thomas J. Pritzker was named chairman of the CSIS Board of Trustees in November 2015. Former U.S. deputy secretary of defense John J. Hamre has served as the Center's president and chief executive officer since 2000.

CSIS does not take specific policy positions; accordingly, all views expressed herein should be understood to be solely those of the author(s).

ISBN: 978-1-4422-8017-5 (pb); 978-1-4422-8018-2 (eBook)

Center for Strategic & International Studies
1616 Rhode Island Avenue, NW
Washington, DC 20036
202-887-0200 | www.**csis**.org

Rowman & Littlefield
4501 Forbes Boulevard
Lanham, MD 20706
301-459-3366 | www.**rowman**.com

Contents

Acknowledgments

This report was made possible by support from a number of institutions and valued colleagues.

I owe great thanks to CSIS for hosting me as visiting fellow in the summer of 2016 to work on this report. Andrew Kuchins extended the invitation to me from CSIS, and Olga Oliker followed up on it. I owe them both a debt of gratitude.

After my arrival at CSIS, Olga's insightful criticism of my work improved the report. Oliver Backes, a master of clarity, line edited my efforts and helped me avoid any obvious embarrassments. Last but not least, I extend many thanks for the diligent interns of CSIS—Mikhail Strokan, Katherine Baughman, Brina Malachowski, and Leland Sidle—for their fact-checking and assistance in tracking details that made this report possible.

Support from the Individual Research Program of the School of World Economy and International Affairs at National Research University—Higher School of Economics is gratefully acknowledged.

In Central Asia and Afghanistan I likewise owe many thanks to friends unnamed here who assisted me in so many ways.

This report is made possible through the generous support of the Carnegie Corporation of New York to the Russia and Eurasia Program at the Center for Strategic and International Studies.

Executive Summary

The general trend in Afghanistan is clear-cut: the overall security situation has consistently deterio-
rated since 2009 and worsened dramatically between 2014 and 2016. However, in the provinces of
Afghanistan adjacent to Central Asia, the security situation has deteriorated even further than in
Afghanistan as a whole on average.

This report considers three security scenarios. In the first, the Afghan National Defense and Security Forces (ANDSF),[1] alone or with foreign support, suppress Anti-Government Elements (AGEs).[2]
As a result, AGEs operate underground, acting as shadow governors primarily in vast village areas.
In the second, the ANDSF and AGE remain engaged in a tense standoff, leading to a de facto
stalemate. In the third, the ANDSF loses out in this standoff to AGEs. This report hypothesizes that
in the second security scenario, which matches current circumstances, core AGEs, namely, the
Taliban, attempt a shift from shadow governance (unofficial rule in many villages) to parallel governance (semiofficial rule from district capitals), which has manifested visibly in some provinces adjacent to Central Asia. If the situation shifts from the second to the third scenario, the Taliban will
solidify their parallel governance.

The immediate Central Asian neighbors of Afghanistan, namely, Turkmenistan, Tajikistan, and
Uzbekistan, are subject to five major security threats originating from the Afghan side of the border:
(1) smuggling by militants; (2) infiltration of extremists; (3) direct Taliban attack; (4) destabilizing
refugee flows; and (5) indirect involvement in the conflict. In the first security scenario, the severity
of these threats would be at an acceptable level (while others would be nonexistent); however, in
the second scenario, they escalate, and that escalation deepens if circumstances deteriorate under
the third scenario. Of particular concern may be the threat of hybrid war waged by the Taliban.

---

1. This is the terminology used by the Special Inspector General for Afghanistan Reconstruction. ANSDF consists of
the Afghan National Army (ANA) and the Afghan National Police (ANP).

2. This is the terminology used by UN Assistance Mission in Afghanistan in order to emphasize that AGEs are more
than just the Taliban.

Consequently, the Central Asians may deem sole reliance on ANDSF for their security insufficient, and they may look to take measures on their own.

The range of available options for Turkmenistan, Uzbekistan, and Tajikistan includes sealing their borders, the creation of nonmilitary or military buffer zones, and direct talks with the Taliban. The report reviews these potential responses and the impact of undertaking them concurrently in a variety of combinations. It is important to note that as some of these measures touch on Afghan territory, they will need to be agreed to with the government in Kabul, and the ability to reach agreement will be dependent on the internal political situation in Afghanistan. Already the Central Asians have entered a sort of "gray zone" defined by a discrepancy between what they may need to do and what the government in Kabul would consider acceptable behavior.

This report concludes that the three immediate Central Asian neighbors of Afghanistan are not content to merely sit behind their borders and rely solely on border protection. They prefer not to meet threats at the border, but rather to actively keep them on the Afghan side without approaching the border. Tajikistan, Turkmenistan, and Uzbekistan have a few options open to them to achieve this goal, but they are limited in their freedom of action. They remain in this "gray zone" of discrepancy between what they need to do and what the government in Kabul will accept. The Central Asians are stuck between unworkable and undesired solutions. This will become a stumbling block for the future political relationship between the Central Asian states and Afghanistan. While this situation may remain in place without any visible effects for some time, it will likely become untenable at some point.

The Situation in Afghan Provinces on the Border with Central Asia

Afghanistan saw dramatic deterioration of its security in the past two to three years. After intense fighting throughout 2015, the government's control of districts in the country was reduced to 70 percent.[1] The Taliban took control of more territory than had been seen since 2001. The Special Inspector General for Afghanistan Reconstruction (SIGAR) report for the first quarter of 2016 was even more pessimistic: "Describing the security situation quantitatively can be difficult. Many numbers are generated, but they are often essentially qualitative assessments using questionable or shifting definitions. And many data points are reported by Afghan ministries with no practicable means of verification."[2] This assessment called into question whether the government in Kabul controlled even 70 percent of districts in the beginning of 2016. The section of SIGAR's report on security was titled "Security: The Erosion of Bedrock," and it systematically outlined a dramatic deterioration of the situation in the country. In each of the next three reports that covered 2016, SIGAR reported further shrinking of governmental control over districts, with an estimate of approximately 57 percent at the end of 2016—a significant depletion over the course of only one year.[3]

Eight provinces located in northeastern, northern, and western Afghanistan border three of the Central Asian states—Tajikistan, Turkmenistan, and Uzbekistan. In the 2000s these Afghan provinces were usually judged to be relatively safe and secure, especially in comparison with the eastern and southern provinces, which have traditionally had a strong Taliban presence. However, this is not true anymore. All eight provinces of Afghanistan on the border with Central Asian countries experience growing insecurity.

---

1. SIGAR, "Quarterly Report to the United States Congress," January 30, 2016, 45, https://www.sigar.mil/pdf/quarterlyreports/2016-01-30qr.pdf.

2. Ibid., April 30, 2016, 5, https://www.sigar.mil/pdf/quarterlyreports/2016-04-30qr.pdf.

3. Ibid., January 30, 2017, 89, https://www.sigar.mil/pdf/quarterlyreports/2017-01-30qr.pdf.

THE BORDER WITH TAJIKISTAN (NORTHEASTERN AFGHANISTAN)

The situation in the Badakhshan region is extremely dangerous. In recent years, two of its districts, Wurduj and Jurm, have been almost completely controlled by AGEs, which also hold considerable territories in other districts. Remote and mountainous, Badakhshan has become a base for AGEs operating in other provinces of Afghanistan.[4] Badakhshan has also become an important "revenue source" for AGEs. There is constant fighting in the Raghistan District, known for its gold- and gem-mining fields. There are also drug laboratories in the province that are practically out of reach of ANDSF and that finance AGEs. Drugs from these laboratories are smuggled through Tajikistan, with these smuggling operations sometimes provoking clashes on the Tajik-Afghan border.

In Takhar, AGEs hold strong positions in the Ishkashim, Yangi Qala, Darkard, and Khwaja Ghar Districts. For several months in late 2015, fighting between ANDSF and AGEs was particularly intense in three of Takhar's districts near the border with Tajikistan—Yangi Qala, Khwaja Ghar, and Darkard. Only in the early months of 2016 was ANDSF able to push AGEs out of the Afghan-Tajik border areas. As usual, AGEs retreated, choosing to conserve their strength for future confrontations.

Most of Kunduz Province is controlled by the Taliban and other AGE groups. The Taliban held the city of Kunduz from September 28, 2015, until October 13, 2015, when ANDSF (with support from foreign troops) forced them into an organized retreat. Their presence in Kunduz city was notable because it was the first time since 2001 that the Taliban was able to seize a provincial capital. The seizure of Kunduz was a clear demonstration of force by AGEs, and the operation allowed them to seize a large amount of weapons, including heavy weaponry. Throughout 2016, ANDSF retained full control of only the central part of the city. In September 2016 AGEs once again attacked Kunduz and retook control, albeit only briefly. Beyond the provincial capital the situation remains volatile in the rest of the province. AGE has heavy influence in all districts of Kunduz.

Tajikistan had been reporting a growing number of border incidents and clashes, in particular in Badakhshan. In the second half of 2015, when the situation deteriorated in Kunduz and Takhar Provinces, the circumstances along the Tajik-Afghan border became significantly tenser. In the fall of 2015, residents of the Panj and Farkhar Districts in Tajikistan's Khatlon region regularly reported to the mass media that their homes were shaking from shell explosions in neighboring Afghanistan and that in some instances shells had landed on the Tajik side of the border (prompting the appropriate apologies offered by the government in Kabul). The Panj River is quite narrow in this area, where the Afghan districts of Yangi Qala and Khwaja Ghar (Takhar Province) border Tajikistan's Panj and Farkhar Districts. Fighting near the border intensified in the fall of 2015, as AGE groups moved into these areas after leaving the city of Kunduz, prompting fears among the Tajik border guard that AGEs could take over this section of the border on the Afghan side. In October 2015 President Emomali Rahmon revealed at a meeting with Russian president Vladimir Putin that AGEs and the

---

4. Armed groups travel through Badakhshan on the way from Pakistan and the eastern provinces of Afghanistan to join up with the AGE group in the northern provinces.

ANA were engaged in fighting on the Afghan side of nearly 60 percent of the Tajik-Afghan border, a circumstance that was of great concern to the government in Dushanbe.[5]

THE BORDER WITH TURKMENISTAN (NORTHWESTERN AND WESTERN AFGHANISTAN)

In Jowzjan Province pro-government forces control the provincial capital and a considerable part of the province. However, AGEs are deeply entrenched in the Kushteppa, Darzab, Aqchah, and especially Khamyab Districts, more or less possessing full control of them. General Abdul Rashid Dostum (an ethnic Uzbek), who became the first vice president of Afghanistan in 2014, traditionally has strong positions in the Jowzjan province and acts as the main security provider there.

The situation in Faryab Province, where General Dostum also has strong positions, is strained. Throughout 2015 and 2016, AGEs not only seized a few district capitals but several times came close to taking control of the province's capital city. Operations mandated by General Dostum against insurgents were initially effective, but afterward retreating AGE fighters regrouped and launched new attacks on the city. Despite some successes, the situation in Faryab continues to be tense, with district capitals under pressure from insurgents.[6]

In Badghis AGEs have strong positions particularly in two districts: Jawand and Murghab. Jawand District borders Ghormach District, administrated from Faryab, and through it other Faryab districts with a strong AGE presence, namely, Kaysor and Almar.

Herat remains a relatively safe province. None of Herat's district capitals were captured by AGEs in the past two years. While AGEs are present in several districts, in particular in Shindand in southern Herat (where they traditionally targeted the American military base in the area), it appears as if the insurgency operating in southern Herat is logistically and administratively more connected to AGEs in the southern provinces in Afghanistan, rather than to northern or northeastern AGEs.

Turkmenistan used to have calm border with Afghanistan, but it experienced a series of minor incidents after May 2013. On February 27, 2014, a much larger incident occurred when an armed group sneaked into Turkmenistan from the Afghan province of Badghis and clashed with Turkmen border guards, killing three, before retreating. Incidents continued throughout the next three years, with militants attacking the Turkmen border from Badghis and Faryab Provinces. The Turkmen government in Ashgabat tried to cover up border incidents, but the governors of the Afghan provinces involved and the Turkmen political opposition reported them. In fact, the concerns of Turkmen officials about the growing insecurity along the Turkmen-Afghan border surfaced

5. "Встреча с Президентом Таджикистана Эмомали Рахмоном" [Meeting with the President of Tajikistan Emomali Rakhmon], Office of the President of the Russian Federation, October 6, 2015, http://www.kremlin.ru/events/president/news/50453.

6. In the summer of 2015, ANDSF managed to detain Mawlawi Salahuddinn, the Taliban governor in Faryab and one of the most notorious Taliban field commanders. However, this detention did not dramatically undermine the Taliban's positions in the province. The new Taliban governor, Mawlawi Zarif, kept most of territories in the Kaysor, Almar, Ghormach, Kohistan, Pashtun Kot, and Gurzaiwan Districts of the province under the AGE control.

publicly through a report by the Afghan president's press service after Hamid Karzai met with the deputy prime minister and foreign minister of Turkmenistan, Raşit Meredow, in May 2014. At the meeting Meredow "pointed to the deteriorating situation in the border areas, particularly the common borders in Faryab and Badghis," and referred specifically to two cases of border clashes in which Turkmen border guards were killed.[7]

THE BORDER WITH UZBEKISTAN (NORTHERN AFGHANISTAN)

Balkh Province of Afghanistan borders all three of Afghanistan's Central Asian neighbors, but its longest stretch of border is with Uzbekistan. In the recent years Balkh Province and its capital, Mazar-i-Sharif, have been subject to an increasing number of terroristic attacks. On April 21, 2017, 10 Taliban fighters disguised in military wear attacked the ANA base near Mazar-i-Sharif, leaving more than 150 killed. Still Balkh is one of the two Afghan provinces (Herat being the other) that border Central Asian countries in which AGEs failed to seize any district capitals in the past two years. This relatively high level of provincial security can be attributed to the governor, Atta Muhammad Nur, who is one of the most influential Tajik politicians and field commanders. He worked to keep the situation under control; however, despite some success, the security dynamic in the province remains negative.

AGE groups set up their bases in the mountains in the southwestern part of Balkh, where the Chimtal, Sholgara, Daulatabad, and Chor Bolak Districts crawled with hundreds of AGE fighters. In these districts, insurgents attempted to build up their strength and create a stronghold for attacks on the provincial capital. Governor Nur personally commanded operations against the insurgents in 2016, which presumably thwarted some of their plans. AGE groups were partially dispersed and contained, but not destroyed. They continue to entrench themselves in the southwestern part of Balkh Province. Although unable to storm and seize Mazar-i-Sharif, AGEs are strong enough to regularly launch terroristic attacks against the city.

Uzbekistan has not experienced direct clashes on its border with Afghanistan, which is well fortified. While minor incidents on the border may occur, the large AGE groups are not able to get close to the border through Balkh Province of Afghanistan. This circumstance does not, however, provide Uzbek officials with any comfort. Uzbekistan observed with a great deal of concern how AGEs mounted forces in the southwest of Balkh, which could lead to future attacks on Mazar-i-Sharif. Furthermore, Uzbekistan was concerned with the situation in Jowzjan and Faryab, which, even though they geographically border Turkmenistan, could serve as a staging group for incursions into Uzbekistan. Militants may in fact prefer a route into Uzbekistan that goes through Turkmenistan, rather than an attack directed at the strong Uzbek border. Even more widely, Uzbekistan views not only these portions of the border but rather its *entire* border with Turkmenistan and Tajikistan as a sort of secondary border with Afghanistan. If armed militants were able to get into Turkmenistan and/or Tajikistan in large numbers, they would be likely to continue on and attack Uzbekistan.

---

7. Bruce Pannier, "Who Do Turkmen Authorities Think They Are Fooling?," RadioFreeEurope, October 20, 2015, https://www.rferl.org/a/who-do-turkmen-authorities-think-theyre-fooling/27316499.html.

THE "BACKYARD" PROVINCES

Until recently Samangan Province was largely safe. It still remains in better security shape than other provinces, but in recent years dozens of AGE groups began operating in the coal-mining Dara-e Suf District.

Sar-e Pol Province is partly controlled by AGEs. AGEs are concentrated in the Kohistan District, where they run a large and well-equipped base (allegedly the best in northern Afghanistan). AGEs also operate in many parts of the Sozma Qala, Sancharak, Sayad, and Gusfandi Districts, as well as in the vicinities of the capital city.

The situation in Baghlan Province has deteriorated dramatically over the past several years. The Taliban position in Tala Wa Barfak District, which is adjacent to the central regions of Afghanistan, is strong, as it is in some other areas of the province where roads to connect Kabul to Kunduz and to Mazar-i-Sharif run. During the seizure of Kunduz in 2015, Taliban warlords managed to hold ANDSF transport for several days on its way from Kabul to Kunduz in the area of Baghlan-e Jadid. Taliban groups possess even stronger positions in Dand-e Ghuri, north of Puli Khumri city, where a road runs between Mazar-i-Sharif and Kabul. After ANDSF failed to return the area to official government control in summer 2015, Kabul authorities signed a deal with local tribe elders that stipulated an end to fighting in the area in exchange for an end to disruptions of transportation along the road. Many observers and politicians in Afghanistan labeled this agreement as a surrender of the strategically important Dand-e Ghuri area to the Taliban. In 2016 ANDSF renewed efforts to regain official control of the area, which reports suggest they achieved March 2016. Even so, the situation in the area remained tense and AGEs strong throughout the rest of 2016.

THE TALIBAN'S QUEST FOR PARALLEL RULE

AGEs and their core Taliban components have already taken strong positions in the eight provinces bordering the Central Asian states. As a result, AGEs in these regions run fortified areas, including training camps and arms depots in districts under their control, which are beyond the reach of ANDSF.

The three provinces referred to above as "backyard," namely, Sar-e Pol, Samangan, and Baghlan, are crucial for AGE operations in the provinces adjacent to Central Asia. Samangan and Baghlan Provinces are important for the integrity of Afghanistan and the ability of the official government in Kabul to govern the northeastern and northern regions.[8] In addition, Sar-e Pol, Samangan, and Baghlan allow AGEs to move their forces between the northeastern, northern, and western provinces of Afghanistan.

It does not appear that AGEs mass their forces in the northeast, north, and west of Afghanistan to fight the government in Kabul. Rather, the Taliban intention may be interpreted as an attempt at taking control of these portions of the country with the goal of establishing their rule in parallel to the official authorities or even, in some regions, prevailing over the official government.

---

8. The main route linking the north of the country with Kabul goes through Samangan and Baghlan. Another road, which also links the northern and central provinces but is less well maintained, also runs through Samangan.

The Taliban takes maximum advantage of the Kabul government's undeclared policy of focusing on securing control over cities, as this policy leaves vast village territories open to the Taliban's shadow governance. However, in the northeastern, northern, and western provinces of Afghanistan, the Taliban's goal is much broader.

It seems that while fighting their way through the eastern and central provinces,[9] AGEs focus mainly on ensuring freedom of movement; however, in the southern and especially northeastern, northern, and western provinces, they seek to entrench themselves and take control of district capital cities there. The Taliban feels safe in districts under their control and are generally regarded by their residents as the authorities. Taliban governors are engaged not only in military but also in social work.[10]

So in the northeastern, northern, and western provinces, the Taliban is attempting to shift from shadow governance (unofficial rule in many villages) to parallel governance (semiofficial rule from district capitals).

---

9. The armed groups that have been forced out of Pakistan over the past few years and joined AGEs have moved across Afghanistan in three directions. First, they moved from Pakistan to Badakhshan directly or through Nuristan, and once in Badakhshan they traveled to Takhar, Kunduz, and Baghlan. Second, they moved from the eastern regions to more central ones, thereby bypassing Kabul in the south and heading northwest to Badghis, Faryab, and Sar-e Pol, or north to Samangan and Baghlan. Third, they traveled via the southern provinces toward the western regions of Afghanistan.

10. The situation in the schools of Kunduz, most of which are controlled by Taliban, is paradoxical but probably not unlike that in other areas under their control. Of the 497 schools in Kunduz, about 300, including 75 in the outskirts of its capital city, are under the Taliban's control. There is an informal agreement between the government, local elders, and the Taliban that these schools are financed by the official government and that the Taliban will not close them. With the exception of arbitrary decisions by the local Taliban leaders in some villages where girls have been forbidden to attend school after the sixth grade, schools continue operating normally, albeit with Taliban oversight and regulation, including through the selection and firing of teachers and the alteration of curricula. For example, the subject "Culture and Civil Education" has been replaced with the study of "A Manual of Islamic Law" by al-Quduri. Taliban mullahs hold daily one-hour classes. In some places they use it to denounce the official regime as godless and to promote other ideology, influencing both pupils and their parents.

02

Security Threats for the Central Asian Neighbors of Afghanistan: A Reality Check

In their public rhetoric, top officials of the three neighboring Central Asian countries have articulated different views on security risks from the Afghan territory. Uzbek officials fully admit the spillover risks,[1] while Tajik officials have slightly downplayed them,[2] and Turkmen officials have bluntly denied them.[3] Despite this diversity in public rhetoric all the three governments detect erosion of security in Afghanistan and apprehend spillover risks, which are basically the same for Uzbekistan, Tajikistan, and Turkmenistan.

There are five major security threats facing the Central Asian neighbors of Afghanistan. Two of these five were live issues even when the International Security Assistance Force (ISAF) mission was in

1. The rhetoric of Uzbekistan's officials can be summarized as follows: they admit instability on Afghanistan's side of the border and see the risks posed by spillover, but remain confident that spillover of this kind is unlikely to affect them given their well-protected border.

2. Tajikistan's officials admit to growing instability in Afghanistan and are cautious about the consequent threats. They have signed on to Commonwealth of Independent States (CIS), Shanghai Cooperation Organization (SCO), and Collective Security Treaty Organization (CSTO) documents that make a similar argument, still the acting authorities are not too vocal about their concerns on the risks of spillover. At the same time, retired officials and mainstream experts maintain in the local press that AGEs are not interested in launching a major attack against the Central Asian neighbors of Afghanistan. Within this logic, the clashes at the border, which are reportedly increasing in frequency, are attributed to criminal and/or radical groups that do not represent core AGEs.

3. Turkmen officials vigorously deny the threat of spillover to Turkmenistan from Afghanistan. One illustrative example of this policy of denial is the diplomatic swordplay between Turkmenistan and Kazakhstan in late 2015. At a joint press conference in October with the leaders of Kazakhstan and Russia, Kazakh president Nursultan Nazarbayev stated: "We already know about the incidents on the border with Turkmenistan and we are concerned about Tajikistan." Just hours later, the Turkmen Ministry of Foreign Affairs publicly protested (in addition to presenting a diplomatic note):

Turkmen side expresses extreme concern and misunderstanding in relation with such a statement by Kazakh side about untrue situation at the state border of Turkmenistan. . . . Turkmen side expresses its strong protest and on

progress, although during that period they stayed at an acceptable level. With AGEs now able to engage ANDSF in tense standoffs, the two threats have escalated and three more have appeared. These threats are likely to further escalate if ANDSF loses the standoff and an AGE establishes its rule in substantial parts of the many Afghan provinces that border Uzbekistan, Tajikistan, and Turkmenistan. The evaluation of these threats and their potential escalation is summed up in Table 2.1, with detailed explanations outlined below.

THREAT A: SMUGGLING BY MILITANTS

The smuggling of drugs and other goods across the Tajik and Turkmen borders with Afghanistan is undertaken with the support of armed groups, often leading to clashes. The Tajik and Turkmen border guards have been dealing with this threat for years, while Uzbekistan has been able to maintain a high enough level of security that the threat from smuggling remains low.

The number of attacks against the borders by militant groups, which serve to provide cover for drug smugglers, has increased in recent years. Coupled with the intensification of fighting between ANDSF and AGEs, the threat posed by smuggling has escalated in a couple of ways.

AGEs, deeply involved in drug trafficking, are gradually taking control of the smuggling business away from other drug dealers, and subsequently fighting for control of new smuggling routes to Tajikistan and Turkmenistan. Additionally, anti-AGE groups may also now need to rely more heavily on illegal sources of revenue to continue their fight against AGEs. If ANDSF loses its grip and regional power brokers begin to play a more prominent role in the war against AGEs, it may also become increasingly involved in drug trafficking or other illegal activities to finance its groups. This will become a particularly serious problem if the international community sharply curtails assistance to Afghanistan. Deprived of this source of financial support, anti-AGE warlords will turn to smuggling or will look to external partners for financial assistance.[4]

As such, AGEs and anti-AGE warlords may both contribute to the escalation of smuggling activity, which is likely to further exacerbate the threat it poses to Tajikistan's and Turkmenistan's borders with Afghanistan (while only moderately increasing the threat posed to Uzbekistan).

The cause of this increased instability is in many ways not just smuggling activity itself but the contentious process of redistributing control of the smuggling business amid the ongoing AGE-ANDSF

---

the basis of traditional brotherly relations between our countries, expresses the hope that in future when assessing the situation around Turkmenistan, Kazakhstan side will be guided by more objective information.

This strong protest, prompted by a mere few words from Nazarbayev, is contradicted by information in the public domain on the many border clashes. See "Press Statements Following Russian-Kazakhstani Talks," Official Website of the Russian President, October 15, 2015, http://en.kremlin.ru/events/president/transcripts/50512; Elena Kosolapova, "Kazakhstan Replies to Turkmen Foreign Ministry's Protest," Trend News Agency, October 17, 2015, http://en.trend.az /casia/kazakhstan/2445056.html.

4. Over the past 15 years of international assistance to Afghanistan, leading politicians and key field commanders have amassed hefty fortunes estimated at hundreds of millions or even billions of U.S. dollars. In principle, key field commanders can fight for some time by drawing on their reserves, but it is highly probable that they will prefer to keep their own fortunes and rely instead on current, including shadow, sources of income.

Table 2.1. Gradation of Threats under Three Security Scenarios

Country	Threat	Gradation of Threats Under Three Security Scenarios		
		Foreigners and/or ANDSF keep AGE down	Tense stand-off between ANDSF and AGE	ANDSF loses stand-off, AGE takes more control
Uzbekistan	Smuggling by militants	low	low	low-medium
	Infiltration of extremists	low	low-medium	medium
	Attack by Taliban	nonexistent	low-medium	medium
	Refugee flow	nonexistent	low	medium
	Indirect involvement	nonexistent	low	low-medium
	Total	2—low	7—low-medium	13—medium
Tajikistan	Smuggling by militants	medium	high	high
	Infiltration of extremists	low-medium	high	high
	Attack by Taliban	nonexistent	medium-high	high
	Refugee flow	nonexistent	low	medium-high
	Indirect involvement	nonexistent	low	medium-high
	Total	5—low	16—medium-high	23—high
Turkmenistan	Smuggling by militants	low-medium	medium-high	medium
	Infiltration of extremists	low-medium	high	high
	Attack by Taliban	nonexistent	medium	medium-high
	Refugee flow	nonexistent	low	medium-high
	Indirect involvement	nonexistent	low	medium
	Total	4—low	14—medium	19—medium-high

Security threats are graded as follows: 1=low; 2=low-medium; 3=medium; 4=medium-high; 5=high. Total for a country is a sum of all grades for an individual threat per country. Each sum is graded as follows: 1–5=low; 6–10=low-medium; 11–15=medium; 16–20=medium-high; 21–25=high.

conflict. If (or when) this redistribution is settled and new smuggling routes are in place, the situation along the borders may stabilize, with fewer incidents (although not lesser flows of drugs). For this reason, the threat posed to both Uzbekistan and Tajikistan does not increase if the AGE is victorious over ANDSF and takes control of territory. In such a situation, the threat posed to Turkmenistan might even decrease somewhat.

THREAT B: INFILTRATION OF MILITANTS

For many years, the threat posed by the infiltration of militants into the Central Asian states was low, as Central Asia saw an outflow of extremists, many of them traveling to fight in Chechnya, Afghanistan, Pakistan, Iraq, or Syria. The Central Asian governments had an interest in having these extremists fight and die abroad rather than remain a threat at home. In the case of Afghanistan, throughout the 2000s the Central Asian authorities sought agreements with the United States and other foreign forces fighting there to target extremists of Central Asian origin. However, the risk of their return could never be wholly dismissed. Some links between extremists of Central Asian origin and their "brothers" in their home regions presumably remained.

Today, the young men who left Central Asia over the past five years with the intention to fight in Syria or Iraq pose a distinct threat. Estimates suggest that approximately 5,000 fall into this category, with others who left Central Asia in the 1990s and 2000s to fight in Afghanistan or Pakistan increasing their numbers further. Their avenues to return home legally are complicated. Some have settled in Turkey or other Muslim countries, while others are reportedly heading to Afghanistan. These fighters may seek to return home by crossing from Afghanistan into Tajikistan or Turkmenistan and subsequently moving throughout the region. Potentially, they could seek the establishment of underground cells in Central Asia and then receive other rebels from neighboring Afghanistan. Of course not all of these fighters will try to return to Central Asia—but some may, and those who do will present a security threat.

THREAT C: DIRECT ATTACK BY THE TALIBAN ON CENTRAL ASIAN BORDERS

In Central Asia, the prevailing opinion is that the core elements of AGEs, the Taliban, have no interest in launching a direct attack against their Central Asian neighbors. This is based on the assumption that the Taliban are fighting with the goal of becoming a ruling power (or at least a partial ruling power) in Afghanistan, and it is therefore assumed that there is zero interest to expand their control beyond Afghanistan's borders. Some Taliban statements support this hypothesis, the latest of which comes from July 2016 and mentions the principle of noninterference in the internal affairs of others. On this basis, the policy of the Taliban is defined as "do no harm nor accept harm," a statement that assures the Central Asian states that under Taliban rule, Afghan territory will not be used as the staging ground for any attacks against neighbors with whom the Taliban, according to the statement, intend to live in an atmosphere of mutual understanding. Interestingly, this statement calls arguments that the Taliban would interfere in neighbors' internal affairs "enemy propaganda."[5]

This risk of direct attack by the Taliban, although perceived as low probability, was always kept on Tajik and Uzbek security radars because of assumed high effects, expected to follow if this potential threat materializes contrary to prevailing expectations.

Currently the assumption that the Taliban does not intend to attack Central Asian borders seems logical and may be true. Still, raids on Central Asian borders from the Afghan territory may not be ruled out even with this general assumption being true. But future intentions of core AGEs are hard to fully predict. Moreover they may shift over time and circumstances.

THREAT D: FLOW OF REFUGEES INTO CENTRAL ASIA

The risk posed by refugee flows was until recently basically dismissed by the Central Asian authorities, as only a few years ago the situation in Afghanistan seemed unlikely to result in such flows. However, with intensifying conflict between ANDSF and AGEs, and with AGEs winning and establishing their rule in district capitals, it is becoming increasingly likely that thousands of Afghan citizens may flee their homes. For the Central Asian neighbors, these refugees will not be "aliens" but rather co-ethnics in many cases. Turkmenistan, Uzbekistan, and especially Tajikistan (where large numbers of ethnic Tajiks from Afghanistan will go) will have to receive at least some of these refugees. These inflows will create not only social but also serious political problems, as well as potential security concerns as militants may attempt to enter amid the flow of refugees. It is also possible that some genuine refugees may radicalize and present a security threat.

THREAT E: INDIRECT INVOLVEMENT IN CONFLICT

Until recently, this risk did not seem relevant. However, with AGEs applying more pressure, the question is what happens if AGEs are successful and force anti-AGE power brokers to retreat. Then they may be interested in withdrawing, at least partially, elements of their rear services support to neighboring territory. Tajikistan, Uzbekistan, and Turkmenistan may receive such requests in this eventuality. Defining a policy in this regard will not be easy, as granting the right to use their territory will mean deeper, although not direct, military involvement in the Afghan conflict.

SYNTHESIS OF THREATS B AND C: FRESH BLOOD TO UNDERGROUND CELLS IN CENTRAL ASIA AND THE PROSPECT OF HYBRID WAR BY TALIBAN

It is important to recognize that the threat scenarios outlined above are not mutually exclusive, and that in reality they may materialize in combination. One particular combination—that of the

---

5. "Afghan Taliban Issues Statement for the Central Asian Countries," *Khaama Press*, July 18, 2016, http://www.khaama.com/afghan-taliban-issues-statement-for-the-central-asian-countries-01509.

infiltration of militants and Taliban attacks on Central Asia borders—may be of particular concern, as it would amount to a new threat of hybrid warfare undertaken by the Taliban.

In this scenario, militants of Central Asian origin infiltrate their home regions from Afghanistan and entrench themselves, most likely in areas remote from the capitals. They are likely to remain in touch with core AGE groups, with whom they fought or with whom they share an ideology, and various foreign sponsors of radical extremism. Inside Uzbekistan, Tajikistan, and Turkmenistan, these militants will go underground and seek out indigenous cells of religious opposition, with the goal of activating them.

It is difficult to get a complete picture of underground activities in Central Asia. In Uzbekistan, the government placed strict controls on the activities of religious organizations in the 1990s, and a lot of radicals left the country in the late 1990s and the 2000s. Even so, 2004 saw a series of terrorist attacks in Tashkent, and in May 2005 a major rebellion broke out in Andijan. Since that time there have been no major incidents involving the local extremist underground. However, the Uzbek security services regularly make arrests on charges of extremist activities. Hundreds of people remain on wanted lists (although many are probably outside the country or dead). Human rights activists suspect that most of the Uzbek government's anti-extremism effort is just an excuse for political repression that uses false accusations of extremist activity as a pretext. While that interpretation is possible, it is also possible that the country's political leadership has ordered the security services to go after radicals and continue hunting for extremists even if no evidence of extremist activity is immediately visible. Supposedly, late Uzbek president Islam Karimov was deeply affected by vivid memories of the strong religious movement his government faced in 1992–1993. The Uzbek authorities worked hard at that time to calm this political uproar, and ultimately to ban the movement and use the full force of the security apparatus to hunt down its adherents, forcing them underground. The Uzbek ruling elite knows better than anyone how large the internal potential for an Islamist-inspired uprising in their country may be. Uzbek authorities manage to keep this threat subdued, so that from the outside the potential for violence seems nearly nonexistent. However, it is their judgment that this is solely due to constant effort and vigilance on the part of the state. The new Uzbek leadership is likely to maintain a similar policy as a result.

The situation in Turkmenistan is in a way like that in Uzbekistan. The state placed strict controls on religious life two decades ago, and at present the official political and public social life is sterilized of radical Islam. However, information on the true state of religious life in Turkmenistan is limited. Turkmenistan appears to have not experienced any uprisings from the local Islamist underground for many years. The last incident that attracted significant attention was in September 2008, when a group of armed people at a factory in northern Ashgabat clashed with police and army forces for two days. Although the battle did not extend beyond this small area, the shooting was so intense that it could be heard in many other parts of the city. After the fact, the government explained away the incident as an operation to defeat a group of drug traffickers; many reject this explanation. A number of unofficial accounts of the incident exist, among them that the security forces were fighting an underground cell of religious extremists. A U.S. diplomatic cable from Ashgabat authored in 2010 discussed the issue of underground mosques in Turkmenistan[6] and confirmed the existence of underground Islamist propaganda in the country, although noting that it was not prevalent.[7] Additionally, members of the Turkmen opposition in exile are vocal on the issue.[8] Throughout 2015 and 2016 these sources regularly reported on increased concern from the Turkmen authorities about the risk of internal Islamic uprising, which has driven them to enact a more proactive, repressive policy meant to detect and eliminate local underground cells. It is important to note that, officially, Ashgabat categorically denies the very existence of this problem in any of its variants. The government denies that there has been a proliferation of unofficial mosques or that Turkmen citizens have traveled to fight in Iraq or Syria. Yet in the late 2000s, the Turkmen government stopped sending students abroad to receive their religious education. As the grand mufti of Turkmenistan explained to American diplomats in 2009, students are now limited to local religious education to keep them away from Wahhabi principles.[9]

The situation in Tajikistan has until recently been fundamentally different from that in Uzbekistan or Turkmenistan; however, recent shifts indicate that the Uzbek or Turkmen pattern may repeat in Tajikistan. The peace accord that ended the Tajik civil war, signed in 1997 by the government and the United Tajik Opposition (UTO), envisioned a governing system that emphasized power sharing. Consequently, many UTO members joined the civil service and security apparatus, though some other UTO warlords, who opposed the peace agreement, remained in Afghanistan and Pakistan in exile. Gradually, the pro-presidential political forces consolidated power and imposed more control on the society and its politics. Even so, for most of the 2000s there was a healthy degree of pluralism in debates on issues of public importance and a number of prominent figures both inside and outside the government who wielded a measure of moral and political authority. These included famous religious leaders and former warlords who did not challenge the government but rather operated quite independently from it. On the whole, this amounted to a model of state stability considerably different from the central government–centric models of Uzbekistan and Turkmenistan. However, starting in 2009 the government began imposing more controls on issues of public life, including religious practice. Furthermore, the government cracked down on former

6. "Wahabis in Turkmenistan?" (cable from the U.S. embassy in Ashgabat, Turkmenistan, February 8, 2010), https://search.wikileaks.org/plusd/cables/10ASHGABAT179_a.html.

7. Many foreign diplomats in Turkmenistan came to believe that there is little evidence of radicalization in the country, though the authorities also prefer not to cooperate with foreigners on the issue and do not reveal any information on the problem to them. As one diplomat explained it in 2010:

> There is little evidence of this in Turkmenistan, however there is an increase in the number of persons attending mosques and an effort by the GOT to increase a sense of nationalistic conservatism which he described as the basis for radicalization. The Turkmen, he said, are not interested in anti-radicalization training because it would be an admission that they have a problem.

See "OSCE Central Asian Mission Heads Striving to Enhance Effectiveness and Cooperation" (cable from the U.S. mission to European Union, Brussels, January 21, 2010), https://wikileaks.org/plusd/cables/10USOSCE15_a.html.

8. This type of source has been regularly reporting on the problem of radicalization in Turkmenistan. Their information is hard in many cases to verify, and is thus inevitably taken with reasonable caution. Still, in no way can it be fully neglected.

9. "Turkmenistan: Das Krol's Meeting with the Grand Mufti—'Turkmen Means Islam'" (cable from the U.S. embassy in Ashgabat, Turkmenistan, April 24, 2009), https://wikileaks.org/plusd/cables/09ASHGABAT522_a.html.

UTO warlords, first those outside of the state apparatus and then those within it. The official and opposition perspectives on the goal of this shift in policy differ greatly. Officials allege ambitions on the part of the former warlords to challenge or even overthrow the government, possibly with the support of their "brothers" in Afghanistan. The opposition, rather, offers a number of theories, including that the government intended to limit or co-opt the business activities of these warlords or even remove them from the picture altogether. The entire opposition agrees, however, that the ultimate goal on the part of the government was to provide a pretext for raiding the UTO warlords. Nearly every year since 2009, the government has conducted operations targeting these warlords in various parts of the country. From May to July 2009, security forces targeted prominent UTO warlords with connections to Afghanistan in the Tavildara region.[10] In 2010 focus shifted to the Rasht region, where former UTO warlords reportedly merged with foreign militants to conduct attacks against government officials, a few of whom had been killed in the region. In both 2012 and 2014 there were security operations in Badakhshan that resulted in the deaths of former warlords, and in September 2015 there was fighting on the outskirts of Dushanbe between security services and a former UTO member, who for many years had been a general in the army.[11] In summer 2015 a high-level active-duty officer, colonel, and chief of Dushanbe police special services disappeared and soon thereafter released a video from Syria, explaining that he went to join the jihad. In September 2015, the Islamic Renaissance Party (IRP), which had been under severe pressure for more than a year and had been left out of the parliament (after receiving only 1.5 percent at the parliamentary elections in March 2015), was banned. Portions of its leadership fled the country, while others were arrested. Some activists were forced underground. Throughout this period, there have regularly been arrests of underground militants throughout Tajikistan, after which the authorities usually publicize their close cooperation with foreign actors. Taken in sum total, these developments indicate that after many years under a power-sharing model that allowed the IRP and former warlords a place in the country's political fabric, the Tajik authorities have finally decided to push them out for good, forcing them to flee, go underground, or end up in prison. This project appears yet unfinished and if pursued will demand further effort from the authorities to sterilize the country's political and social life from any form of religious politics or radicalism.

In summation, the authorities in Uzbekistan and Turkmenistan seem to believe that, speaking figuratively, the fire of Islamic radicalism has gone out, but its smoldering remnants are also dangerous and need to be constantly fought. That is why officials invest unlimited time and effort into keeping the radicals deep underground. Security services detect and kill those that surface, but survivors hide even deeper. Security services always assume that there is still something beyond

---

10. In this region official security forces primarily targeted and ultimately killed Mulla Abdulla, who had not admitted the 1997 peace agreement, stayed in exile in Afghanistan and Pakistan, and reportedly returned illegally with a group of fighters to the Tavildara region of Tajikistan, which had previously been his stronghold. Another famous former warlord, Mirzo Zieev, was also killed. He had admitted the peace agreement, served for many years as head of paramilitary ministry of emergency, and from 2007 had lived in a home in Tavildara on retirement. In 2009 he reportedly took the side of Abdulla.

11. This general Abduhalim Nazarzoda made a career in the official army up to the position of deputy minister of defense. In 2015 he joined a group of fighters that reportedly attacked governmental forces in Dushanbe and neighboring Vahdat region, where he was traced and killed.

their reach. If they cannot extract that from underground and eliminate it, they prefer to push it even deeper into the underground. Tajikistan, which once seemed genuinely different, is now following a similar trajectory, pushing all radicals and their sympathizers underground. This is despite arguments on the part of the IRP leadership that their place in the formal political process helped divert this energy away from radicalism into efforts to address the problems affecting people's lives (and, potentially, the root causes of radicalization in the first place). While the Tajik authorities presumably understood this argument, they chose the path of Uzbekistan and Turkmenistan. The increasing destabilization of Afghanistan was likely an important factor in their decisionmaking, alongside, of course, Syria and the larger phenomenon of the Arab Spring. The leadership of the Central Asian governments and their security apparatuses intend to throw cold water on the smoldering remnants of radicalism at home and bar the door against fresh blood that might join the fight.

Militants coming from or through Afghanistan are exactly the fresh blood that these governments fear. If such an inflow occurs in substantial quantity and quality, local underground cells may recover and at some point rise up, especially in the territories accessible from Afghanistan (such as the eastern regions of Turkmenistan, the southern regions of Uzbekistan, the eastern and central parts of Tajikistan, or even the southern Kyrgyz and Uzbek portions of the Fergana valley). Such a rebellion, of course, could not succeed on its own, and the local security services are confident in their capacity to quash a local uprising. The concern, then, is that the goal of such a rebellion would be to gain the support of the main AGE groups in Afghanistan who could come join the fight.

Core AGEs in Afghanistan are likely stand in solidarity with their ideological brothers in Central Asia in such a circumstance. Even analysts that take at face value the Taliban's stated commitment to noninterference in Central Asian affairs are likely to admit that the Taliban is by no means monolithic, and that there would thus be debate within it regarding the question of supporting Central Asian radicals. A number of moral, financial, and other considerations would ultimately drive AGE decisionmaking in this regard, with the end result being potentially clear-cut support for their "brothers," a refusal to intervene, or official neutrality with allowances for individuals to act in their individual capacity as volunteer fighters. This third scenario would lead to what is sometimes referred to as "hybrid war," which may be even worse for the neighboring Central Asian countries than a direct and open assault by the Taliban.

03

Central Asian Policy Options

The Central Asian neighbors of Afghanistan have a number of possible responses to the threats outlined above. This spectrum is limited by two opposite extremes: relying on ANDSF and the central government in Kabul or sealing off their borders with Afghanistan even at the expense of cultural and economic contacts (with minimal exceptions, such as for humanitarian aid). Between these two extremes lie three other major options: cutting a deal with the Taliban, creating a military buffer zone, or creating a nonmilitary buffer zone on the Afghan side of the border.

RELYING ON ANDSF

In 2015 and 2016, ANDSF faced a tough challenge from AGEs. By all reports, ANDSF experienced serious casualties over this period, with at least 19,000 wounded and killed in 2015,[1] a 25 to 30 percent year-on-year increase. Furthermore, the killed-to-wounded ratio is alarming at approximately 40 to 60 percent, and these significant losses inflicted by AGEs drove up desertion rates

---

1. The United Nations, referencing information from Afghan authorities, reported 12,168 casualties (4,541 deaths and 7,628 injured) for January–October 2015 with the note that figures for the last two months were unavailable "due to reporting restrictions imposed by the Government at the end of 2015." SIGAR, referencing the U.S. military in Afghanistan, reported for all of 2015, 6,637 killed and 12,471 wounded, for a total of 19,108. It is not possible for the November–December gap to account for the nearly 40 percent discrepancy between these two reports. And while the UN and SIGAR use different terms, the UN definition of ANDSF is not narrower than SIGAR's ANDSF. A media report that referenced an unnamed NATO source estimated total Afghan army casualties (included the wounded) at 15,800 in 2015. What should be considered is that per the U.S. military: "The ANP (Afghan police) have sustained a disproportionately higher number of casualties than the ANA (Afghan military)." Together ANA and ANP constitute ANDSF. This usual disproportionality in ANA and ANP losses even further complicates the aforementioned discrepancy. If only ANA casualties were about 15,800, then total ANDSF casualties should be above 30,000. However, if total ANDSF casualties were 19,108, then the ANA casualties should be below 10,100, which, if true, would contradict all reports regarding the severity of the fighting. There is, however, another explanation for this discrepancy. As SIGAR testifies: "Neither the United States nor its Afghan allies know how many Afghan soldiers and police actually exist." It is a long story of inconsistency in payroll lists and actual number of soldiers and police on duty. The discrepancy in number of casualties indirectly proves that probably ANP numbers are far below what has

(which were not low to begin with). Even during the ISAF mission, desertion rates were estimated at 20 percent per year. In 2016 at least a third of the ANA was composed of first-year soldiers. While there is still considerable recruitment potential, these new recruits are minimally effective, requiring significant training before joining the fight. Such a level of rotation is unsustainable.

There is yet another factor that must be considered. As the fighting has intensified, ANDSF has had to use indiscriminate heavy weaponry, such as artillery, resulting in a significant rise in the number of casualties among civilians at the hands of ANDSF and, in particular, ANA. The UN, which tracks casualties in Afghanistan, has reported in nearly all past years that AGEs were responsible for more than 70 percent of deaths and injuries among civilians (and in some years, such as 2012, an even higher percentage—80 percent). However, 2015 was both unusual and pivotal: the AGEs were responsible for only 62 percent of civilian casualties and ANDSF for 17 percent (compared with 9–11 percent before).[2] In 2016 the trend continued: the AGEs were responsible for 61 percent and ANDSF for 24 percent.[3] These figures are disquieting for Kabul. If this trend continues, public support for ANDSF may erode.

While ANDSF is operating at the end of their tether, it is equally critical that they do not possess strong political backing. The atmosphere of mistrust and suspicion inherent in Afghan politics has, if anything, been amplified by the frozen political crisis that has lasted since the flawed 2014 presidential elections. This atmosphere feeds, and then in turn is reinforced by, widespread rumors in political circles and the mass media about "double-dealing" by high-level government officials. Throughout 2015 and 2016, Afghan political circles have been buzzing with rumors that certain Afghan politicians and officials are involved in the redeployment of AGE groups to the north of the country, and in secret deals with the Taliban and other AGE groups, including Daesh.[4] In the first days after an AGE's capture of Kunduz city in September 2015, a former head of the Afghan National Security Service, Amrullah Saleh, claimed that Kunduz's fall was the result of conspiracy with participation of top Kabul officials, although he declined to name them.[5] At the same time, opposition members in the

---

been reported. See UN Assistance Mission in Afghanistan and UN Office of the High Commissioner for Human Rights, "Afghanistan: Annual Report 2015—Protection of Civilians in Armed Conflict," Kabul, Afghanistan, February 2016, https://unama.unmissions.org/sites/default/files/poc_annual_report_2015_final_14_feb_2016.pdf; SIGAR, "Quarterly Report to the United States Congress," April 30, 2016, https://www.sigar.mil/pdf/quarterlyreports/2016-04-30qr.pdf; Sayed Sarwar Amani and Andrew MacAskill, "Desertions Deplete Afghan Forces, Adding to Security Worries," Reuters, January 18, 2016, http://www.reuters.com/article/us-afghanistan-army-desertions-idUSKCN0UW1K3.

2. The decrease of AGE responsibility and increase of ANDSF responsibility was not proportional. The UN decided not to attribute civilian casualties from fighting in Kunduz in October 2015 either to AGEs or to the ANDSF, leaving those casualties unattributed; see UN Assistance Mission in Afghanistan and UN Office of the High Commissioner for Human Rights, "Afghanistan: Annual Report 2015—Protection of Civilians in Armed Conflict," Kabul, Afghanistan, February 2016, 31, https://unama.unmissions.org/sites/default/files/poc_annual_report_2015_final_14_feb_2016.pdf.

3. UN Assistance Mission in Afghanistan and UN Office of the High Commissioner for Human Rights, "Afghanistan: Annual Report 2016—Protection of Civilians in Armed Conflict," Kabul, Afghanistan, February 2017, 6, https://unama.unmissions.org/sites/default/files/protection_of_civilians_in_armed_conflict_annual_report_2016_16_feb_2017_final.pdf.

4. "MP Zahir Qadi Claims Daesh Commanders Live in Kabul," *Khaama Press*, November 23, 2015, http://www.khaama.com/mp-zahir-qadi-claims-daesh-commanders-live-in-kabul-4353.

5. "Амрулла Салех: Кундуз пал в результате заговора с участием должностных лиц" [Amrullah Saleh: Kunduz Fell as a Result of a Conspiracy with the Participation of Officials], Afghanistan.ru, September 30, 2015, http://afghanistan.ru/doc/90118.html.

parliament speculated about the existence of "a fifth column" (also referred to locally as "Taliban members with ties") well established in the presidential administration.

These allegations are mentioned not to endorse them, but rather to illustrate how tense the debate is within Afghan political circles and serious deficit of trust that prevails. President Ghani, who now suffers a great deal as a result, partially contributed to the creation of this circumstance himself.[6] Ghani pushed forward his policy of negotiations with the Taliban and implemented it in a nontransparent way that to some seemed borne from a lack of political will to fight, rather than other considerations. Although in summer 2016 Ghani revisited his position on reaching a deal with the Taliban, the atmosphere of mistrust and suspicion between various parts of the anti-AGE political class remains and will further undermine ANDSF.

SEALING THE BORDER WITH AFGHANISTAN

Tajik, Turkmen, and Uzbek policy toward their respective borders with Afghanistan has changed considerably from the 1990s to today, a transition that has seen countries that initially sealed themselves off from their southern neighbor come to the conclusion that addressing security concerns on the Afghan side of the border was critical. As a result of this shift, border protection itself was viewed by all these countries as not an end in and of itself, but rather as the means to hedge against failures of other more attractive options.

Turkmenistan perceived a relatively minimal threat emanating from the Afghan side of the border. The Turkmen government chose to defend its border with Afghanistan largely without much reliance on force. Both Turkmen presidents have pursued a policy course reliant on a mixture of economic projects (some time shadow) and diplomacy. Uzbekistan lies at the other extreme, heavily investing in robust border protection. Those doing business between Uzbekistan and Afghanistan have been forced to adapt to strict border controls, for example. Tajikistan's policy falls somewhere in the middle. While Dushanbe was attracted to the potential benefits of cultural reconnection to the

---

6. In some cases, Ghani's choices of high-ranking officials raised a lot of suspicion among his political opponents. The figure of former acting defense minister Mohammed Masoom Stanekzai, who stayed in the office from spring 2015 to summer 2016, was particularly controversial for many. Stanekzai received a military education (he graduated from a military school in Kabul as a signaler), but his career had little to do with the military, as he instead served as a human rights commissioner and a minister of communications. In Karzai's team he was one of the staunchest advocates of talks with the Taliban and took practical steps to organize them as a member of the High Peace Council and an internal security adviser to the president. In July 2015 members of the Wolesi Jirga (House of the People, or lower house of parliament) refused to confirm Stanekzai's appointment as defense minister, citing his lack of professional experience as the reason. However, the main reason was that on September 20, 2011, being the head of the High Peace Council's Secretariat, Stanekzai escorted a Taliban suicide bomber to a meeting with former president of Afghanistan and High Peace Council chairman Burhanuddin Rabbani (an ethnic Tajik from Badakhshan, a deeply respected figure in Afghan politics and especially among former Northern Alliance members). Rabbani was killed, Stanekzai was injured, but many remained suspicious of him thereafter. And yet President Ghani kept Stanekzai, his fellow man coming from the president's native province of Logar, as acting defense minister for over a year. See K. I. Iskandarov, "Pravitel'stvo nacional'nogo edinstva v Afganistane" [National Unity Government in Afghanistan], *Bol'shaya Igra: politika, biznes, bezopasnost' v Tsentral'noi Azii* [Great Game: Politics, Business, Security in Central Asia] 44, no. 5 (2015): 21–22.

Persian space and the strategic economic opportunities to its south, it continued to prioritize border protection. The story of Tajikistan's policy toward Afghanistan has been that of a search for a balance between reliable border security and the development of economic and humanitarian ties.

So Central Asian neighbors pursued border protection quite differently. This applies to not only the resources and effort put toward border protection but to the management of this policy more broadly. Uzbekistan has focused on reinforcing its own security capabilities and pursuing when necessary bilateral cooperation with Russia or the United States. Turkmenistan has prioritized and relied on assistance from the United Nations. Tajikistan combines reliance on its national forces to combat lower-level border threats with cooperation with the CSTO to face down security risks beyond its national capacity.

As these countries have witnessed growing instability in Afghanistan, they sought for more international cooperation to support their national border protection. Uzbekistan has sought to expand cooperation with Russia in this area, though on a strictly bilateral basis.

Tajikistan has also broadened cooperation with Russia bilaterally and the CSTO multilaterally, restarting these dialogues in 2010 and 2011 after a period of decline in cooperation in the late 2000s. Still Dushanbe refused to allow Russian troops to be redeployed along the border.[7] Tajikistan is prepared to sacrifice some economic ties with Afghanistan in exchange for ensuring security.[8] Border protection has been tightened in recent years, provoking complaints among Afghan entrepreneurs. The Tajik authorities were particularly alarmed in the fall of 2015, when there was fighting in Afghanistan within 10 kilometers of the border. While by spring 2016 the fighting had moved away from the border, the Tajik border guards reportedly remained on high alert.

From 2014 through 2016 Turkmenistan has been working to fortify its border with Afghanistan. However, as a result of a legacy of insufficient investment in maintaining the relevant infrastructure and training personnel, they are likely to experience difficulties moving forward. While the Turkmen authorities deny that there are any problems relating to their capacity to protect the border, there is evidence to the contrary. Turkmenistan is seeking out partners to increase its capacity, with reports in 2014 outlining Turkmen contacts with Turkey and Uzbekistan on the issue. Turkmenistan has also discussed military cooperation with Russia[9] and the United

---

7. There is a version of events that proposes that Tajikistan's decision was prompted by the U.S. position. See George Gavrilis, "Afghan Narcotrafficking: The State of Afghanistan's Borders," East-West Institute, April 2015, 22, 23, https://www.eastwest.ngo/sites/default/files/ideas-files/Afghanistan-Borders.pdf.

8. I. A. Safranchuk, "Tadzhikistan i Turkmenistan: raznye podhody k zashhite granicy s IRA" [Tajikistan and Turkmenistan: Different Approaches to Protecting Borders with Islamic Republic of Afghanistan], *Bol'shaya Igra: politika, biznes, bezopasnost' v Tsentral'noi Azii* [Great Game: Politics, Business, Security in Central Asia] 45, no. 6 (2015): 39.

9. The Russian minister of defense planned to visit Ashgabat in 2015, but his visit was delayed presumably at the initiative of the Turkmen government. Sergey Shoygu later traveled to Ashgabat on June 9, 2016. He met the Turkmen president and minister of defense and reportedly discussed, in broad terms, counterterrorism, arms sales, and training. While the Turkmen-Afghan border was not mentioned in Russian or Turkmen news coverage of this visit, observers are certain that it was the primary subject of negotiations. See "Главы оборонных ведомств России и Туркменистана обсудили военное сотрудничество и проблемы региональной и глобальной безопасности" [Heads of the Defense Ministries of Russia and Turkmenistan Discuss Military Cooperation and Problems of Regional and Global Security], Ministry of Defense of the Russian Federation, June 9, 2016, http://function.mil.ru/news_page/country/more.htm?id

States.[10] It seems that Turkmenistan faced unexpected political roadblocks in its search for external assistance to improve its national border protection capabilities. General Lloyd J. Austin III, commander of U.S. Central Command, testified to the Senate Armed Service Committee on March 26, 2016, that "Turkmenistan's declared policy of positive neutrality limits our opportunities for substantive military-to-military collaboration." The ultimate U.S. response to Turkmenistan's request for U.S. military equipment and technology to address threats at the border with Afghanistan has been, simply, "We will do what we can to support those requests."[11] It is not yet clear how Turkmenistan will accommodate substantive military cooperation with foreign partners to its neutrality policy.

In summation, Uzbekistan can seal its border with Afghanistan and faces little in the way of political or economic constraints in implementing such a policy. However, Uzbekistan does not believe that further closure of an already well-policed border would ultimately improve the security situation. Tajikistan, meanwhile, can seal its border only through greater cooperation with Russia, up to and including an agreement to return Russian military forces to the border. Dushanbe has hesitated to pursue such a policy because of a number of political and economic considerations, and like Tashkent does not see this as the ultimate solution to their security problems. For Turkmenistan, sealing its border with Afghanistan is an extremely difficult task in technical terms, which could be done only through close military cooperation with a capable partner or partners that would potentially compromise its political neutrality. Besides, Turkmenistan also does not believe that sealing the border is the ultimate solution and wants to keep avenues open for mutually beneficial economic projects with Afghanistan. As such, sealing the border with Afghanistan is presently at best the option of last resort. All other options would have to prove insufficient for Tajikistan, Turkmenistan, and Uzbekistan to pursue this policy, or for the political calculus within these capitals to change dramatically. Border protection, of course, will continue to be emphasized by all three governments, but still as a hedge against failures of other more attractive options.

CREATING A MILITARY BUFFER ZONE

In the late 1990s Uzbekistan and Tajikistan both had experience in supporting anti-Taliban mujahedeen on the Afghan side of the border. These were members of the anti-Soviet insurgency in the 1980s, many of them with background of religious opposition back in the 1970s, who headed the Afghan government formed in 1992 after the collapse of the pro-Soviet regime. The Taliban

=12086971@egNews; "Министр обороны России генерал армии Сергей Шойгу был принят Президентом Туркменистана Гурбангулы Бердымухамедовым" [Russian Defense Ministry and General Sergei Shoigu was received by the president of Turkmenistan Gurbanguly Berdimuhamedov], Ministry of Defense of the Russian Federation, June 9, 2016, http://function.mil.ru/news_page/country/more.htm?id=12086969@egNews.

10. General Lloyd J. Austin III, commander of U.S. Central Command, stated to the Senate Armed Service Committee on March 26, 2016, that "the Turkmens recently expressed a desire to acquire U.S. military equipment and technology to address threats to their security along their southern border with Afghanistan." See Lloyd J. Austin III, "Statement of General Lloyd J. Austin III, Commander, U.S. Central Command, before the Senate Armed Services Committee on the Posture of U.S. Central Command," March 26, 2015, http://www.armed-services.senate.gov/imo/media/doc/Austin_03-26-15.pdf.

11. Ibid.

overthrew this government in 1996, but its key members formed the United Islamic Front for the Salvation of Afghanistan, widely known as the Northern Alliance. It resisted the Taliban rule in Afghanistan and was primarily non-Pashtun (with a prevalence of Tajiks, Uzbeks, and Hazaras), but some prominent Pashtun warlords also joined it. Members of the Northern Alliance kept calling themselves mujahedeen. After 2001 such anti-Taliban mujahedeen joined new governmental structures of Afghanistan and converted into politicians. However in the late 2000s, with the Taliban insurgency growingly successful, mujahedeen started dwelling on the question of whether to renew their political-military alliance on the basis of patronage networks and militia they kept maintaining at home regions. With each wave of instability in the northeastern, northern and western provinces of Afghanistan, where mujahedeen traditionally have most influence, this issue comes more and more to the forefront.

In 2010 the Taliban struggled to increase its influence in northern Afghanistan and targeted prominent non-Pashtun figures, killing more than a dozen of them in 2010 and 2011. The most famous victim was Burhanuddin Rabbani, head of Peace Council and the former president of Afghanistan, who was assassinated in September 2011. In response to that Taliban's assault, mujahedeen formed the National Front, which at that time was informally referred to as the New Northern Alliance. It sought to carve out a place in Afghan politics and also develop support from abroad, but it failed. At that time, key mujahedeen leaders chose to stay in close alliance with President Karzai and not to oppose the government in Kabul.[12] In the fall of 2012, Ismail Khan, former governor of Herat, gathered some mujahedeen in Herat and presented a strong warning of the imminent escalation of the conflict with the Taliban and blamed Kabul for its reluctance to respond effectively or prepare for war. While meetings and discussion in this vein continued, this initiative went nowhere as well, as the strongest field commanders and mujahedeen politicians hoped to retain their positions in the official government in Kabul. They became actively involved in the election campaign in 2013 and 2014. Ghani's victory and his actions as president have prompted mujahedeen to continue to consider a political-military alliance.

The new wave of instability in 2015, in particular the seizure of Kunduz city, drove mujahedeen to become vocal once again. In December 2015 Abdul Sayyaf declared a Council for Protection and Stability in Afghanistan that brought together key mujahedeen leaders, many of whom had held senior positions during Karzai's rule. However, after an auspicious start the initiative did not develop to much. There is a lack of unity among the mujahedeen as they are struggling internally for resources, influence, and authority. There are also ethnic contradictions between the Uzbek and Tajik mujahedeen groups. Among Tajiks themselves, who traditionally played a big role in anti-Taliban mujahedeen's movement, there is not enough unity. All this impedes efforts to renew some meaningful mujahedeen military-political structure.

Even more importantly Kabul opposes efforts by mujahedeen and their militia to take on the responsibility for security anywhere in the country. In both 2015 and 2016, President Ghani authorized operations led by his first vice president General Dostum and acting governor Nur in

---

12. The position of Mohammad Qasim Fahim, the first vice president in Karzai's second presidential term, was important on this question. Some other prominent mujahedeen, like Nur and Mohaqiq, showed interest in the National Front at first but then distanced themselves from it.

provinces, where they respectively wield considerable influence. Even still, Ghani reasserted a policy of centralized responsibility for security and made clear that these few exceptions did not change the policy in general. Visiting Kunduz city shortly after it was freed from the Taliban in October 2015, when the central authorities fell under harsh criticism, Ghani stated: "Militia forces will not be formed under any circumstances and responsibility to individuals will be delegated in a professional setting."[13] In these circumstances the majority of mujahedeen seek to solidify their positions in the Kabul government rather than oppose it. This is the only way for mujahedeen to legalize their influence in the home regions.

Therefore, the mujahedeen with their militia groups are currently unable to assume full responsibility for security in the northeastern, northern, and western provinces of Afghanistan. The neighboring Central Asian countries are unwilling to create political tension with Kabul by supporting regional warlords in open contradiction to Ghani's clear-cut policy. This status quo is likely to remain in place as long as the official government in Kabul functions, retaining international recognition and internal legitimacy.

CREATING A NONMILITARY BUFFER ZONE

In the 1980s, it was clear to Soviet specialists that if the local communities in the Afghan areas adjacent to Central Asian borders benefited from stability, then they themselves did not contribute to security problems and in fact acted to constrain those that might otherwise pose a security risk. Recognition of this dynamic contributed to decisions to provide humanitarian assistance, like food and medical supplies, to these populations along the border, a practice that continued during the 1990s, when Russian border guards were stationed on the Afghan border in Turkmenistan and Tajikistan. At present, the idea of pacifying local communities through the provision of assistance is being considered once again in an expanded way, as the creation of a "nonmilitary buffer zone."

The rationale behind such a policy is twofold. First, the Taliban enters into certain arrangements with local communities in the districts that it controls. If locals have a stake in maintaining peace along the border, it is likely to be part and parcel of their deal with the Taliban, in which they agree not to undermine the peaceful management of the border. Second, local communities may be so interested in maintaining border peace that they would forcefully resist attempts to attack a border by forming a local, grassroots militia. Both of these arguments have merit.

These arrangements are likely to be even more solid when the local communities have more than just practical common interests with cross-border sponsors. Uzbekistan, Tajikistan, and Turkmenistan all have ethnic compatriots in the border areas on the Afghan side. Common language and cultural traditions provide an opportunity to underpin humanitarian assistance with educational and other soft-power initiatives. This may create even more incentives for local communities to keep the peace along the border.

---

13. "President Ghani Visits Kunduz Province and Assesses the Situation," Office of the President, Islamic Republic of Afghanistan, October 16, 2016, http://president.gov.af/en/news/president-ghani-visits-kunduz-province-and-assesses -the-situation/.

Unlike a military buffer zone, a nonmilitary buffer zone policy is unlikely to lead to too many controversies with the Afghan central government in Kabul. Though Kabul insists on channeling all big projects in the country through the central authorities, humanitarian and other soft-power projects, which are unlikely to be source of large revenues, are something Kabul may allow to be managed locally.

All of Afghanistan's Central Asian neighbors may consider a nonmilitary buffer zone strategy in Afghanistan, building on a history of traditionally providing humanitarian assistance. Such a strategy may be seen as attractive by Tajikistan and particularly by Turkmenistan, as it has not favored particularly tough border protection policies to date and may as a result favor soft-power policies to pacify the population on the other side of the border. Turkmenistan's behavior to date suggests that such a policy is preferable to Ashgabat. In fact, Ashgabat is increasingly active in shaping such a nonmilitary buffer zone, with Tajikistan likely to contribute at some point to a similar effort.

After the incidence of accidents on the Turkmen-Afghan border escalated in 2014, Turkmenistan's minister of foreign affairs traveled to Kabul to discuss cooperation between the security services to prevent future violence. President Karzai agreed to more security cooperation on the border, but also blamed "external forces" for the clashes, which could be interpreted as the Afghan government admitting to a limited capacity to improve or even affect the situation in the border areas. After clashes on the Turkmen-Afghan border continued in 2015, Turkmen representatives started traveling through provinces of western and northern Afghanistan, meeting with regional and local authorities to discuss humanitarian and economic assistance. Turkmenistan also started hosting these regional and local authorities for, presumably, establishing good relations (although this practice is largely hidden and not regularly reported in the public domain). In 2016 this effort continued with the involvement of high-level political players with Raşit Meredow, deputy prime minister and foreign minister of Turkmenistan, visiting Faryab, Jowzjan, and Balkh Provinces.

MAKING DEALS WITH THE TALIBAN

In the late 1990s, after nearly a decade of instability in Afghanistan, all its immediate Central Asian neighbors realized that it was necessary to reach agreements with the Taliban, which by that time controlled most of the country. Today, after more than a decade of foreign military presence in the country, Tajikistan, Turkmenistan, and Uzbekistan have to consider the option again. While the standoff between AGEs and ANDSF continues, these countries may pursue ad hoc agreements with individual field commanders on certain issues. Yet if the Taliban establishes parallel semiofficial rule in Afghanistan, they could pursue much broader security and political agreements with the Taliban's leadership.

All three of Afghanistan's Central Asian neighbors have previously been in contact with insurgent groups in Afghanistan, with Turkmenistan possessing the most robust history in this regard. They are likely to run limited agreements with Taliban field commanders through their national secret services or some other underground, nonaffiliated facilitators. However, if any broad deal with the Taliban's leadership is to be pursued, all the regional countries, in particular Turkmenistan, will seek the UN's active involvement both legitimate the negotiations and preserve their diplomatic reputation.

SYNTHESIZING THE AVAILABLE RESPONSES

Of the potential responses outlined above, none of them alone (save an unworkable reliance on the ANDSF and an undesired full closure of the border with Afghanistan) will respond to security concerns effectively enough on its own. Therefore, any workable strategy to respond to the security challenge posed by Afghanistan will need to combine elements of multiple of these responses.

As the threat grows amid the ANDSF standoff with AGEs, the Central Asian states are paradoxically ready to become more involved on the Afghan side of the border to help keep threats away from their borders, rather than to barricade themselves behind their national borders. As such, they are likely to pursue a policy of sponsoring both nonmilitary and military buffer zones on the Afghan side. However, the further escalation of the threat, particularly in the scenario when ANDSF lose out to AGEs, may lead the Central Asians into another paradox, namely, a desire to make deals with the Taliban while still endeavoring to keep threats away from their borders, rather than fighting them at the border. As such, negotiations (either limited or broad, but preferably direct) may be added on top of efforts to build nonmilitary and/or military buffer zones. At the same time, all three countries will continue to increase their border protection efforts out of concern that the situation could deteriorate further.

These four responses—nonmilitary buffer zones, military buffer zones, deals with the Taliban, and more focus on border protection—are likely to be the most attractive for Afghanistan's Central Asian neighbors. However, each will probably combine them in different proportions. Turkmenistan already invests enthusiastically into nonmilitary buffer zones. Tajikistan is also likely to consider this option. Uzbekistan, however, will be more restricted in this regard and may not go beyond providing standard humanitarian assistance. At the same time, Uzbekistan and Tajikistan may closely consider sponsorship of military buffer zones, while Turkmenistan is unlikely support such an effort.

THE "GRAY ZONE" DISCREPANCY BETWEEN SECURITY THREATS AND THE ABILITY TO RESPOND

Uzbekistan, Tajikistan, and Turkmenistan can only dream of being absolutely insulated from threats from Afghanistan. In reality, they will need to find a comfortable balance between the threats they face and their capacity to address them. Of course, in circumstances where these responses touch Afghan territory, the Central Asian governments cannot do just what they please, but rather must limit themselves to what Kabul finds acceptable. The latter is dependent on developments in the internal political situation in Afghanistan. There are three issues that are critical in this regard: Does Kabul maintain legitimacy through an internal political crisis and the next slate of elections? Does it reach a peace agreement with Taliban? And does it grant more freedom of action to regional power brokers or maintain centralized rule? The answers to these three questions will determine the types of Central Asian activities Kabul will accept.

The below options, dependent on the political situation inside Afghanistan, are summed up in Table 3.1.

Table 3.1. The Gray Zone of Insecurity

	Policies Central Asian Governments May Need to Implement		Policies That Kabul Will Accept from Central Asian Governments	
	if the prevailing expectation is that Taliban will not attack	*if the prevailing expectation is that Taliban will attack*	*Depending on state of government in Kabul, then . . .*	*Kabul will accept the following policies . . .*
Security Scenario 1: Foreigners and/or ANDSF keep AGE down	Relying on ANDSF	Relying on ANDSF, More border protection	Kabul gov. stays legitimate, with or without deal with Taliban; doesn't give more freedom to regional warlords	Relying on ANDSF, More border protection
Security Scenario 2: Tense stand-off between ANDSF and AGE	Nonmilitary buffer zone, More border protection, Deals with Taliban (limited, direct) Military buffer zone (modest investment in it)	Nonmilitary buffer zone, More border protection, Deals with Taliban (limited, direct) Military buffer zone (up to serious investment in it)	Kabul gov. stays legitimate, no deal with Taliban; gives more freedom to regional warlords	Nonmilitary buffer zone, More border protection, Military buffer zone (modest investment in it)
			Kabul gov. stays legitimate, deal with Taliban; doesn't give more freedom to regional warlords	Nonmilitary buffer zone, More border protection, Deals with Taliban (through Kabul gov.)
			Kabul gov. stays legitimate, no deal with Taliban; doesn't give more freedom to regional warlords	Nonmilitary buffer zone, More border protection

(Continued)

Table 3.1. The Gray Zone of Insecurity (Continued)

	Policies Central Asian Governments May Need to Implement		Policies That Kabul Will Accept from Central Asian Governments	
	if the prevailing expectation is that Taliban will not attack	*if the prevailing expectation is that Taliban will attack*	*Depending on state of government in Kabul, then . . .*	*Kabul will accept the following policies . . .*
Security Scenario 3: ANDSF loses stand-off, AGE takes more control	Nonmilitary buffer zone, More border protection, Deals with Taliban (from limited to broad, direct) Military buffer zone (up to serious investment in it)	Nonmilitary buffer zone, More border protection, Deals with Taliban (from limited to broad, direct) Military buffer zone (up to serious investment in it) or Sealing off borderline	Kabul gov. stays legitimate, no deal with Taliban; doesn't give more freedom to regional warlords	Nonmilitary buffer zone, More border protection
			Kabul gov. stays legitimate, deal with Taliban; doesn't give more freedom to regional warlords	Nonmilitary buffer zone, More border protection, Deals with Taliban (through Kabul gov.)
			Kabul gov. stays legitimate, no deal with Taliban; gives more freedom to regional warlords	Nonmilitary buffer zone, More border protection, Military buffer zone (modest investment in it)
			Kabul gov. loses legitimacy, de facto loses power in most of the regions; regional warlords take more responsibilities	No limitations from official Kabul

A balance between Central Asian security needs and Kabul's conditions is easily achievable if the ANDSF is able to keep AGEs down. In this scenario, the security risks for the Central Asians are relatively low (see Table 2.1) and they can rely on ANDSF to keep threats away from Central Asian borders. Importantly, in this case a balance between Central Asian needs and Kabul's conditions exists only because of the limited necessity of action on the part of the Central Asians. But the present situation has already diverged from this scenario.

Currently, ANDSF is engaged in tough standoff with AGEs. Being unable to keep AGEs down, ANDSF still may be capable of maintaining the status quo, denying the Taliban an opportunity to establish semiofficial parallel governance through the capture of district capitals. While ANDSF may not be fully successful with this task, it is not doomed to failure in the short run. Within this scenario, the risks for Central Asia increase (as outlined in Table 2.1) and they have to take additional measures (outlined in Table 3.1). However, Kabul may not accept some of these measures.

The central government in Kabul is likely to agree to only two types of actions by the Central Asians on Afghan territory: a light version of a nonmilitary buffer zone (which in reality may look very much like humanitarian assistance, but with some conditionality to local communities and regional authorities) and the implementation of more border protection measures (it is impossible for Kabul to oppose measures taken on the Central Asian side of the border). Even so, Kabul is likely to attempt to keep these policies modest in their scope and implementation. The central authorities in Kabul will struggle to keep conditionality for humanitarian assistance at the lowest possible level, which will add difficulties for efforts to convert humanitarian assistance into the creation of a nonmilitary buffer zone. Kabul will also pursue further economic cooperation and the development of transportation links with Central Asia, which is likely to stimulate complaints from business communities on too-tough border protection. This narrative may curb efforts for a real sealing-off of the borders.

Kabul is likely to block other measures more actively. As long as Kabul maintains its political legitimacy, it will always oppose and impede direct contacts between the Central Asians and the Taliban. Kabul will also oppose or block any attempts to develop a military buffer zone. Kabul will accept some versions of a military buffer zone only if it agrees to some decentralization and grants more responsibility for security to regional authorities and regional militias. But this is exactly what Kabul strongly rejects.

There is obviously a major discrepancy between what the Central Asian countries may need to do and what Kabul will accept. This discrepancy defines the "gray zone" of imbalance between the threats to the Central Asians and their ability to respond to them—a gray zone that the Central Asians find themselves in today.

Within the current security situation, this gray zone could have been avoided if Kabul had agreed to some decentralization and placed more responsibility for security on regional power brokers and their militias. This would have provided an opportunity to build robust nonmilitary buffer zones and support them with a military buffer zone, assuming some of the Central Asian states choose to do so. Together with more border protection, this would meet security needs of Central Asians. Even so, some of them would also look for limited, direct contacts with Taliban. However, as said above, Kabul is not prepared to allow for decentralization.

Under the current security scenario, Central Asians would also avoid the gray zone if Kabul had made a deal with Taliban. This could have eased security pressures and given the Central Asians an opportunity to enter into direct talks with the Taliban, although Kabul would have still opposed them. But so far Kabul has failed to reach an agreement with the Taliban.

Consequently, in the current security scenario, the Central Asian countries are already deep in this gray zone of discrepancy between threats to them and their ability to react. But they will move even farther into it if ANDSF fails to maintain the tense standoff with AGEs and gives Taliban a chance to establish a parallel rule from district capitals in the regions of Afghanistan adjacent to Central Asia. In this case, the security risks they face will further escalate. Consequently, the Central Asians will need to take additional measures, such as a robust military buffer zone or engaging in direct talks with Taliban's leadership, even though Kabul will continue to strongly oppose them. As such, the gray zone will only widen.

The level of threat facing Central Asia and the scope of their responses are interdependent. Kabul must either decrease threats originating from the Afghan territory or lift internal political restrictions for Central Asians' actions. If Kabul allows threats on its territory to escalate and limits the Central Asians in their responses, this pushes neighbors deeper into the gray zone. Eventually the situation could deteriorate to the degree that, from the Central Asian perspective, the net utility of the legitimate government in Kabul may become negative. This would occur if ANDSF is losing to the AGEs, but the central government remains politically strong and does not enter into power-sharing arrangements with regional anti-AGE warlords or, on the contrary, the Taliban, or somehow with both of them. In this case Uzbekistan, Tajikistan, and Turkmenistan must meet the growing threat and are yet restricted in their potential responses, which may lead them to welcome the collapse of the central government in Kabul with the removal of all limitations on their freedom of action.

Consequently, it is in the interest of Kabul government to eliminate this gray zone in order to maintain full support of their Central Asian neighbors. Kabul may do this through either dramatically increasing the capacity of ANDSF to defeat or tamp down AGE activities or through power sharing with Taliban (which would end most of the fighting), or regional warlords and their militias (which could then act autonomously and may cooperate with Afghanistan's neighbors).

04

Conclusion

The situation in Afghanistan has deteriorated as ANDSF has failed to keep AGEs down and is now engaged in a tense standoff. Within this security situation, the Taliban, after many years of practicing shadow governance primarily in vast village areas, is trying to establish parallel semiofficial rule from district capitals, while the central government in Kabul remains focused on preventing this. Kabul's priority is now to keep the Taliban from occupying district capitals, something ANDSF has been able to do so far, although the prospects for permanently defending all of them look bleak. These efforts to establish parallel rule are particularly visible in southern Afghanistan and the provinces adjacent to Central Asia.

This is of great immediate concern to Afghanistan's Central Asian neighbors. They face a number of escalating threats, including smuggling by militants, infiltration by extremists, direct attack by the Taliban, increased flow of refugees, and indirect involvement into the conflict. Some of these threats in combination may result in a hybrid war by the Taliban overlapping on both Central Asian and Afghan territory, even though the prevailing perception in the region today is that the Taliban will not go beyond Afghan borders.

For many years, Uzbekistan, Tajikistan, and Turkmenistan relied on foreign troops and ANDSF to secure Afghanistan and when AGEs were kept down, this was sufficient to meet their security needs. These neighbors hoped to benefit from a secure Afghanistan and the new economic opportunities that presented. However, the Central Asians do not want to share in Afghanistan's insecurity. Their basic interest is to store problems on the Afghan side of the border, preferably with a buffer zone between them.

Their options in pursuing this desired end state are numerous. Between the two extremes of relying on ANDSF to reimpose security and the full closure of their borders, Turkmenistan, Uzbekistan, and Tajikistan have a few options: the creation of nonmilitary and military buffer zones and direct talks with the Taliban. Each of Afghanistan's three Central Asian neighbors may pursue these policies in different combinations. Turkmenistan is already building a de facto nonmilitary buffer zone along its border with Afghanistan, and Tajikistan may do so, while also considering a military buffer zone. Uzbekistan is likely to consider a military buffer, while Turkmenistan will not. All these countries may be interested in direct talks to Taliban. At the same time, all of them are focusing more attention and resources on border protection. However, they do not believe in border protection as an ultimate security solution in and of itself. Border protection remains for them the strategy to hedge against failures of other more attractive options.

In considering a policy of nonmilitary or military buffer zones and direct talks to Taliban, the Central Asians will have to take into account the position of Kabul, whose view on these issues is dependent on the internal political situation in Afghanistan. Already now there is a "gray zone" of discrepancy between what Turkmenistan, Uzbekistan, and Tajikistan may need to do and what Kabul would accept.

The situation is paradoxical. Central Asians would like to rely solely on ANDSF, but they cannot do so as its ability to sustain security is questionable. However, they cannot take any other measures to keep threats on the Afghan side of the border because of official Kabul's objections. Thus, they are pushed to invest more into border protection, up to and including efforts to seal the border, which they do not want to do.

The Central Asians are stuck between unworkable and undesirable options. Theoretically they could choose to assist the Afghan government to increase the capacity of ANDSF or enter into open political conflict with Kabul to force it to tolerate their policies that affect Afghan territory and impinge on Afghan sovereignty. Yet the former is unlikely to be effective and the latter not desirable. As such, they find themselves again between the rock and the hard place of unworkable and undesirable policy options.

This "gray zone" is the principal stumbling block for political relations between the Central Asians and Afghanistan. Turkmenistan, Uzbekistan, and Tajikistan may remain in this limbo for a while, reluctant to clash with Kabul or isolate themselves from Afghanistan by sealing the border. While the standoff between ANDSF and AGEs remains stable, the Central Asians will probably prefer this limbo, easing the situation for Kabul, which would likely continue to receive regional support. Even so, a discrepancy between stated positions and real security interests may emerge and is likely to continue to grow over time. With further security deterioration, the central government in Kabul may become a hindrance, if it does not enter into power-sharing arrangements with regional anti-AGE warlords or with the Taliban. In this scenario, Kabul may quickly lose support from its Central Asian neighbors.

About the Author

Ivan Safranchuk graduated in 1998 from the Moscow State Institute of International Relations (MGIMO) and in 2003 received the degree of candidate of sciences (the Russian equivalent of a PhD) from the Academy of Military Sciences, where his work focused on post–Cold War nuclear strategy. From 1997 to 2001, he worked at the PIR Center for Policy Studies, including as director of the Nuclear Arms Control Project. In July 2001 he opened CDI Moscow, a Russia-based branch of the U.S.-based Center for Defense Information; it was renamed the World Security Institute (WSI) in 2006. Since 2008 Dr. Safranchuk has served as an adviser to WSI while focusing on his private consulting work.

Since 2003 he has lectured at MGIMO in Moscow, and since 2016 also at National Research University–Higher School of Economics. Since 2007 Dr. Safranchuk has published a magazine entitled *Great Game: Politics, Business, Security in Central Asia*. From 2011 to 2014, he served as deputy director of the Institute of Contemporary International Studies at the Diplomatic Academy of the Russian Ministry of Foreign Affairs. He has been a member of the Advisory Council to the Center on Global Counterterrorism Cooperation since 2011; a member of the Council on Foreign and Defense Policy (SVOP), a community of leading Russian security experts, since 2012; and an adviser to the president of the Diplomatic Academy of Kyrgyzstan since 2015. In 2016 Dr. Safranchuk was a visiting fellow with the Russia and Eurasia Program at CSIS and in 2017 a Rice Faculty Fellow with the MacMillan Center at Yale University, teaching a course on Central Asia.

Over the past nine years, Dr. Safranchuk has been involved in many projects related to Central Asia and Afghanistan. These include research projects for Russian, U.S., and European organizations and also for international organizations, including the United Nations. He has authored publications on nuclear strategy and arms control, nonproliferation, Central Asia, and Afghanistan.

www.ingramcontent.com/pod-product-compliance
Lightning Source LLC
Chambersburg PA
CBHW081438270326
41932CB00019B/3249